LIVE YOUR
TRUTH

KAMAL RAVIKANT

LIONCREST
PUBLISHING

For Werner

PREFACE

Somewhere along the way, you do your best, and then you surrender. Let go. Of attachment to outcomes. Attachment to what you desire. Like a paper lantern you light and then release into the night sky.

You do your best, you let go.

It is not powerlessness. It is freedom. Like you're in a dark room and it's bright outside. Surrender means cleaning the window so that light can enter. You're letting the light enter, not making it enter.

It is not giving up, it is accepting. And the light will enter. Always does.

Despite how we may rock the world, we have our weak point. That one thing that can bring us down. For me, it's the end of love. I know I'm not the only one.

I wrote this book over a period of two months after a painful breakup. On one hand, life was zipping. Things and opportunities I'd wanted for long were happening easily. On the other, the Achilles' heel.

I was doing my practice, loving myself. But the mind was resisting, refusing to let go. So I wrote. Night after night. True sentence after true sentence. I wrote for myself, to myself. A handbook, a guide. Reminders of what I know is real, what I know that works. So as the pain went away, I would be left behind with these records of truths.

If ever in pain, I think the best thing we can do is to create something. A record. Not of pain, but of what is real. Pain doesn't last. And when it's gone, we have something to show for it. Growth. And because it is a human experience, it is of value. Something we can share with others.

This book guided me back to my truth. Light naturally flowed in. I let go of outcomes and returned to working on being my best self. And that is the greatest gift I can ask for.

SAIL AWAY

LIVE LONG ENOUGH and you start to see patterns in your life. The seasons and the storms. The way that things work for you, the way that they don't.

In the winter of 2012, I spent the last week of December at a monastery in Big Sur, high up in the hills overlooking the Pacific. No talking. No internet or cell phones. The sound of rain on the roof my companion

A new year was coming. Rather than resolutions, I wanted to approach it from an effective place. A place of inner knowing, of lessons learned. The desire was to write down what I know that works — what makes me healthy, what makes me productive, what fulfills me, the basics of what makes my life zing — and then live it.

I'd written a little book that summer called *Love Yourself Like Your Life Depends On It*. Published it on Amazon, expecting to sell ten copies, max. It took off and became a success. Word of mouth, blog posts, tweets. The book has a life of its own, spreading around the world.

If anything, the book was a gift to me. It made me cross a threshold, showed me that my voice mattered. Sharing my truth mattered. My life mattered.

I got many emails from readers, mostly those who applied what I wrote about, how it improved their lives. But there were some that had a difficult time. They couldn't do the love yourself thing. Something was holding them back.

It happened to a friend I'd shared the practice with. She tried everything under the sun — accepting herself, trusting herself, liking herself — anything but love. No matter how much I shared what had worked for me, she wouldn't go there.

When you have an answer and you see someone you love struggle with the question, it can drive you batty. I could share what I knew, but never force it. So how to get her there?

And here's what I realized. Loving myself, that was my truth. Something I discovered from within myself. And because it came from inside me, there was no denying it. I couldn't forget about it, rationalize it away. I had no choice but to live it.

I had to guide her to find her own truth. And she found multiple. Loving herself, being an example for her children, the gifts she wants to express to the world. Her life, she tells me, is vastly different than before. She's taken risks, made changes in her career, her health, and even how she lives her days. Things she hadn't thought possible, hopes that she had buried away. Amazing opportunities she never expected are happening naturally. Not surprising. The truth is a part of her in ways she can never hide. She lives it. Rocks it.

In the end, we are human beings with human minds having human experiences. No different from each other or those who came long before us. The scenery might differ, but the basics stay the same. A truth you learn or a process you use can apply to anyone. That's the beauty of life. The answers are always available.

At the monastery, I set out to write how to be better on the outside. But as is the nature of creation, what resulted was far different. Habits and goals and success are just details. The tip of a deep iceberg. What matters is the foundation, the stillness below the surface. The truth inside. Living it, the rest is a natural byproduct.

I hope that this book inspires you to investigate yourself, discover your own truth. When something comes from within, when it is a part of you, you have no choice but to live it, to express it. That's when you become, well, awesome.

There is one rule, though: once you discover your truth, you have to go all in. Fully. Every single chip.

That is when the shift happens. As if there's a force in life waiting for us to make the decision, to commit, jump off that cliff. Then life breathes a deep sigh and opens the gates, fills the sails.

It's magical to experience. I wish that for you.

THE SAMURAI

HIGHWAY 1 LEADING TO the monastery is closed due to storms. Rather than a three and a half hour trip, I drive almost six hours through back roads, switchbacks deep in the hills, sharp corners and turns, and occasional rockslides.

You'd think that this would be the best way to be present, to be in the moment. But the mind is active. A friend I lost this year, the company I built for four years and just shut down. Memories of a breakup still fresh. Thoughts coming and going, patterns of thoughts, loops upon loops. The mind pauses to hit the brakes, avoid a deer, then returns to the chatter.

I reach the monastery and check into my cold cement cottage. Technically, it's called a monk's cell, and is located in a row of similar cottages where the real monks live. There is a bathroom smaller than my car, an alcove for meditation, and a cubby for the one-person bed. About as simple as it gets.

I turn on the stove for warmth, unpack, and pull out a book I brought with me, *The Book of Five Rings* by Miyamoto Musashi, the greatest swordsman in Japanese history.

It's a beautiful copy. Hardback, calligraphy. Written in the seventeenth century near the end of his life, it's Musashi's core teachings. I read it years ago and still remember simple lines that, if applied to one's life, would transform you. It's that kind of book.

Like many of his contemporaries, Musashi was also a talented painter, sculptor, and poet. Unlike his contemporaries, he was self-taught. Everything he knew, he had learned himself. His craft, hardened by battle. Action, not theory.

The man fought more than sixty individual matches and three major battles. If anyone has honed the mind to serve in the moment rather than distract, it would be him. So it's not surprising that while the book is about swordsmanship and strategy, it's also about the work within. About eliminating fear.

Throughout the book, at the end of each section, he repeats only one phrase: You should investigate this thoroughly. If you could boil his teachings down to one thing, that would be it. And I understand. Knowledge is never enough. Even action, if it's just following a prescribed way, will never fully express your potential. But to dive in, test each theory out, kick the tires, keep what works, discard the rest, add your own — that's where magic happens.

I put the book down and stare out the window. The rain has stopped. I have seven days to go and already, the world seems so far away. I zip up my jacket and go out to explore.

OPENING

Late night, sitting on a wall at the outer edge of the monastery. Feet dangling above the ocean far below. A low fog hugs the coast. The air, cold and crisp. The moon so bright, I almost have to shield my eyes.

I used to think that loving myself was an inside job. I still do. The mistake I made was that if there were low points, I'd love myself through them alone. It worked most of the time.

But I've learned that to reach out, be open and vulnerable to what I need, almost like a child, that is loving myself too. Perhaps the simplest, the most honest, the most loving thing I can do for myself.

One day I did. My mind was so intent in loss after the breakup, so unwilling to let go, that I grabbed my phone off my desk and texted a friend.

"I'm hurting."

She texted right back. "How can I help?"

I didn't let myself think. No second-guessing, no time for fears to erect walls.

"Tell me that you love me. Tell me that I am loved."

It was iMessage, so I could see the empty speech bubble. Apple's servers telling me that she was typing.

"I love you."

I stared at the screen. Speech bubble appeared. New text.

"You are so loved."

That's all I needed. I had no idea. That's all I needed.

I walk around, a man in this society, big strong adult mask on. Seeming to have it all together. Sometimes true. Sometimes far from it. There are times that even my best isn't enough. I will stumble, I will fall. And those times, the best thing I can do is reach out to someone who truly loves me, ask them for help, to hold out their hand.

I think that each of us has our own personal evolution. I tend to figure things out by myself. So my evolution would be to involve others, grow with them. For someone who's wired to figure things out with others, their evolution would be to go within alone. Either way, we evolve and meet in the middle. Comfortable in the silence within, comfortable with reaching out.

I don't have life figured out. But I sure am trying my best. If I fall, to learn from it so that when I rise, I have the gift — the lesson — that I absorb into myself and share.

This lesson was a hard one. But it's moved me so much further, created such deep and profound relationships, that I can't imagine being another way. Sometimes, the only way to evolve is to open ourselves fully. Be raw, honest. Vulnerable.

That's another thing I've learned. There is strength in this vulnerability, in tearing down the walls. People sense it in you. The world is hungry for it. And the greatest healing — for you, for those around you — it comes from opening. Opening yourself wide. To your humanness, to your feelings. And ultimately, to yourself.

.

PILLARS

I'm in my cottage, reading Musashi. The old bell rings, announcing Vespers. The monks live structured days, prayers four times spread out from morning to evening, each announced by the bell.

"Put this into action," Musashi says of his teachings. "Surpass today what you were yesterday." I shut the book, go stand outside and breathe in the evening. The rain stopped at sunset but you can feel it hanging around, ready to return.

What are the key components of one's life? Buckets, that if you fill daily, even if just a drop, move you forward and create progress. So that who you'll be months from today will be vastly better in all the ways that count.

James Altucher has his daily practice, four buckets to fill: mental, spiritual, physical, emotional. According to him, if you meet those each day, your life will be transformed. And I believe him. When you search for truth within, and then you see it outside yourself, you know instinctively if it will work for you.

A talented entrepreneur told me the four categories that he works on: health, wealth, relationships, and self-expression. I believe that too. When you are healthy, not lacking, have great relationships with those that matter, and express who you are through your work or your family or your art or whatever that is important to you, you are truly living.

One thing I've learned: we don't stumble accidentally into an amazing life. It takes decision, a commitment to consistently work on ourselves. The best ones I know, like the two above, they do it daily. A focused practice. They fail, but they pick themselves up, continue forward. If there is any secret, that is it. And over time, the days blend into a life that amazes the world.

RHYTHM

It feels late but I'm not tired. Outside, pitch dark. The cottages, quiet. I check the time and it's barely ten. Life works on a different schedule at the monastery. I put on layers, go for a walk.

I can't remember the last time I saw so many stars. Or heard such silence. But not in my head. The world I left behind just two days ago still bounces around my mind. Lots happened in the past year. Beginnings and endings, opportunities and goodbyes.

"There is a rhythm to everything," Musashi wrote. "To music, battle, even mounting a horse. You cannot ignore it. Rhythm to being in harmony with others, and a rhythm to not being in harmony with them."

If I could add to it: a rhythm to being in harmony with oneself.

Life happens. Series of events occur. Some I judge good, some I judge bad. Some I want to have happen, others I don't. The latter, I usually fight against in my mind, wishing they weren't so. The former, I wish for more.

Love, pain, fears, hopes, dreams, desires. All arise from the mind. We're stuck in our heads, walking around, reliving old stories and patterns and beliefs. The ever constant human drama. I don't know why our brains are wired that way, they just are.

But knowing that helps me immensely. I know that regardless of the situation or whatever the external experience is, I choose who to be in this moment. I choose what to feel in this moment. Often it feels like we're on autopilot, but if you examine your thoughts closely, you'll know that not to be true. It is always a choice.

So I work hard on myself to make conscious choices moment by moment, day by day. It is a practice. There is a rhythm to it. I fail often. I fail spectacularly. But there are times when I succeed and each moment of success is a reinforcement, a new thought pattern I'm laying down. One that serves me, makes me better, makes me who I want to be.

Here's what happens: when I change my mind, my world changes. If you think about it, makes sense. When your sense of self and happiness comes from within and isn't a roller coaster ride dependent on others or circumstances, you approach life differently. You make better choices. You draw to you the people and situations that matter. The others, they fall away.

A lone pair of headlights weaves along the highway below. I stop, watch the car until it is out of sight, then stare up at the stars.

When I was five years old, I spent a year living with my grandmother in New Delhi. We would spend the hot humid summer nights sleeping on the roof. It was common practice. Aunts and uncles and cousins would join, laying out cots and blankets on the cement. They'd talk and joke and laugh and slowly, one by one, we would grow quiet and then it was just crickets and the occasional sound of someone on the street.

The stars, I remember the stars, how they covered the sky. Each night, I'd try to count them, thinking that if I really tried, I could number them all. There were a lot, but not so many that a dedicated five-year old couldn't tackle. And that's how I'd drift off to sleep. Counting stars, losing track, starting over, counting stars.

Never seemed to bother me though. There was a patience, a knowing that the exact number didn't matter. What mattered was that I saw the stars, one by one, as I lay on my back and explored the sky.

These days, living in a city, it's rare that I see a sky full of stars. A few here and there, but that's about it. On a night like tonight, when I'm away from civilization and I see the glittering sky above, rather than counting — I know it's impossible and for some reason, that stops me now — I think of the light reaching my eyes. What I'm seeing existed millions of years ago. I'm looking at the far far past.

And out there, beyond the haze of the Milky Way, galaxies and nebulas, and more galaxies, so many, our rock just a minor speck of sand in the beach of the Universe. When I think of that, I think of myself, so tiny and brief, and yet, who I am, the potential of me so big and vast.

Whether accidental or designed or a cosmic joke between green aliens, the human experience is an unbelievably amazing one. Our ability to love and create — that alone makes this entire experiment worthwhile.

Moments like this, I feel the rhythm of my life. The ups and downs, the intense beauty of it all. My life is a piece of music, and if I look at it that way, knowing that pitch is a crucial component, it naturally calms the mind down. And I can't help but be grateful for it — for this crazy ride that I somehow signed up for.

I may not be able to change someone. I may not be able to change a circumstance. But I can change myself, how I respond, who I am being. That is where all the power resides. Inside.

A shiver passes through me. I wrap my hands around myself, rub my sleeves for warmth. So many stars. For a moment, I'm tempted to count them all. I smile and walk back to the cottage.

WERNER

My friend Werner passed away four months ago. I found out on Facebook, heading out the door to catch a flight. A quick message someone posted on his wall. He'd had a heart attack at the gym. That's it. Gone.

I remember sitting on that plane, open sky through the window, processing the news. The hardest part, I'll never see him again. That classic full laugh of his, how he always had fun wherever he went, whatever he did. If there was a guy who lived life on his terms, he was it.

Tall, bald, the biggest grin. First a DJ in London, then a promoter, then a kite surfing instructor in the Caribbean, then a talented silversmith. Whatever he decided he wanted to do, wherever he decided he wanted to live, he just went and did it.

If there's a definition of freedom, I think it's this: living life on your terms. And Werner was the freest man I've known. I miss him terribly.

Outside the cottage, rain. I close my eyes, listen to it, and imagine him sitting across from me.

"I'm sorry, man," I say.

"Ah," he waves his hand at me. Smiling. "Let it go."

We're both quiet for a little bit.

"Reach out to Siv once in a while," he says, "and Ice." Siv, his wife. Ice, his dog.

Rain picks up, drums on the roof.

He smiles, slow. "But they'll be gone too." Long pause. "And you. Life, it is quick."

Life is long, a chain of intertwining moments, looping round and round. But life is short. Blinks. Memories. Connections. Then you're gone.

The truth: I live my days as if I will live forever. Putting off so much, expecting there to be more time, another chance. If I accepted my mortality to my core, never knowing when the chain snaps, then how would I live?

More on my terms. A free man. I'd write more, I'd love more, I'd laugh more.

Can I succeed at it, this way of living? I don't know. But I will remind myself daily: I am mortal. I will feel gratitude for it. For another opportunity to be here, to live and love and hurt and play and create and make good and bad decisions. Life.

I have a hunch that my journey, however long it plays out, shall be better for it.

Thank you, Werner.

WHAT IS TRUTH?

Perhaps better to start with what truth isn't. It is not experience. It is not a story or label or the kaleidoscope of our lives. It is never what we did or what someone did to us.

In college, I had a breakup that devastated me. My first love. It was the worst thing I could have imagined. Looking back, it's one of the best things that ever happened to me. The relationship was long over, it was my insecurities that were desperately hanging on.

Neither the breakup nor my interpretations of it over time are real. They are just neurons firing, paths across synaptic connections. The stories we weave to make sense of this journey of ours.

What we do and experience, those are like fireworks in the night sky. Sometimes pretty, sometimes scary, lots of booms and oohs and aahs. Flash, bang, gone. None lasting, none real.

What is real is the one within who watches these fireworks. The inner self, it knows truth.

Truth doesn't change. It is the real you, regardless of your life story. Truth is what heals you, what saves you. Truth makes you rise to new heights, no matter where you are.

The thing is, we're human beings living our lives, doing the best we can. No one dropped us off with instruction manuals. No, if in situation X, flip to page 243 and choose solution Y. Life is a series of choices and all we can do is make them.

Sometimes we'll choose ones that serve us, sometimes not. And when that happens, it's our duty to be gentle with ourselves. We are human. We will make mistakes.

It's the nature of our being. Sometimes we'll look back at those mistakes as the best things we ever did. That's also part of the contract.

That is why it's crucial for us to find our truth, to own it. Your truth is the core lesson. The guiding star. Knowing it will naturally help you with your decisions, the paths you choose to take. That's the practical application of your knowledge.

And when life seems out of control — you will have a foundation, an anchor to return to. To be still. To know what is real.

The magic is that as we live our truth, life does seem to calm down, as if that's all it needed from us anyway. To be our real selves.

TECHNIQUE

THE BAD NEWS: there is no one simple technique for finding your truth.

The good news: there is no one simple technique for finding your truth.

No twelve step program. Or bulleted list. No seventeen new proven scientific ways, auric healings, or quantum attunements for a limited time for $99.95. There is not an app for truth.

If any did exist, I'd be wary of them. The human condition is too vast and beautiful for such things. Instead, what you have is freedom.

Ask yourself: what is it, that if I believed it down to my core, would change everything? Make the fears irrelevant? Make the person I'd become so unbelievably amazing that I'd blow my own socks off?

Answer that, and you're on your way.

For me, it was loving myself. For one friend, feeling worthy. That transformed his life. For another, abundance. Opportunities literally throw themselves at him. For many, I've seen it to be their faith.

The only rule is that truth must empower you, make you better in every way possible. That's it.

You can pick it out of a book, a sermon, a movie, a conversation, a passing remark, a thought while running on the beach. You can discover it in the stillness within. All are valid. It is your life, your experience. Your truth must feel right for you.

Once you decide on it, the requirement is a commitment to live it fully. Not hope. Hope may get us out of a rut, but it will not transform. Only fierce action, doing whatever it takes. Knowing that we will fall often, but we will pick ourselves up, move forward, keep our commitment to ourselves because it is the most important one there is.

The good news: it gets easier as you do it.

The bad news: you must continue to do it. Even when you don't want to. Especially then.

CHAIN

A RECENT MEMORY...

Hard Rock hotel, late night, walking back to my room. Pass photos of famous musicians, stop and stare at them for a while. Kurt Cobain. You can see the pain in his eyes. I look at others, similar. Do all artists have to suffer?

Part of me resists when I ask the question. I don't want the answer to be yes. But I let go, and the answer, instead, is of a different sort. They have to experience. To live and experience life fully because when you create art, if it's not true and real, you know.

Hemingway, Cobain. Both killed themselves. But what if they hadn't? What if they'd gone with the experience, whatever they were feeling, whatever they were fighting, knowing that it too would pass, and left behind would be the knowledge, the gift they could put into their art?

With the wisdom of age, what else could Hemingway have written? And Cobain, perhaps he might be a poet today or even just another burned out rocker. But whatever he'd created, as long as he stayed true to his experience, it would have connected and changed lives. Just those two, what could have been…it's sad, I will never know.

I'm old enough to have lost friends. Random deaths are tough. Suicides, the worst. I've also lived long enough to look back at those gone and know that whatever they were dealing with, it passed. They didn't have to. They could have been here, wiser and stronger and better.

No matter how smart we may think we are, no matter how committed we are to our truth, we can lose our way. We're human. Made of flesh and feelings, not armor. And knowing that, there is something we can do to let in the light when we're fighting it the most.

Set the ego aside. Reach out, share your truth, tell someone, "This is who I am. This is what I stand for. Hold me to it." Be accountable. Often, we'll do far more for another than we will do for ourselves. Use that to your advantage.

Once, while meditating, I saw an image of my parents standing in front of me. Behind them, their parents. And their parents, and their parents, and their parents. An unbroken line of lives so long that it faded into the horizon. An unbroken line of lives that ultimately led to mine.

Then I thought of those who have touched my life. Minor and major ways. And all the lives that were lived so that just these few could exist and walk the Earth with me for a brief spark in time. Lines upon lines, connections upon connections, ripples spreading across time and generations. Humanity doing its dance so that you could be here, reading these words I just wrote.

Even if we may feel like it sometimes, we are never alone. I write this, expecting that you will read these words. I write them with the hope that they will improve your life. I am giving you my all. My truth. That you will read it is a gift to me. I may never meet you, but that's ok. I smile, knowing that we are links in a beautiful chain connected in ways deeper than we can imagine.

Whatever you experience in your life, choose for it to make you grow in amazing and unbelievable ways. You owe it to yourself. You owe it to those who came before you. You owe it to those connected to you who you'll never meet. You owe it to those who have yet to come into your life.

SUCCESS

I LOVED MYSELF. My company failed. I loved myself through it. There were tough moments, laying off employees, looking investors in the eye — many of whom were close friends — and telling them that I was sorry. I was broke and in debt. I loved myself through it all.

It wasn't easy. Loving yourself, sometimes it is puppy dogs and rainbows. Other times, it's not. And that's when it's needed the most. I loved myself through the tough moments.

Here's what happened. I sat down and wrote a little book, sharing something from the heart. Put it out to the world. It spread wings, took off. I watched in wonder as it flew, developing a life of its own. By all standard metrics, it became a hit.

I received emails daily from readers thanking me, how it touched them, and a few telling me it had stopped them from killing themselves.

Whoa.

How do you take in something like that?

If my company had not failed, the book would not have been written. And if the book had not been written, one of those lives might have gone.

This experience has shattered my definition of success forever. How do you measure saving a human life?

Before I got sick and learned to love myself, I played around with the thought of suicide. On the real tough days when the company was tanking, I'd sit in the office at night, working, staring at the Bay Bridge through the windows, fantasizing about jumping off. It was a delicious thought.

After I learned to love myself, those thoughts went away. Then, when the book came out, to hear that it did the same for others, that is the gift they gave me. And it continued, opening doors, creating opportunities that I never could have predicted.

Now I know what success is: living your truth, sharing it. Whether through a book, raising a child, building a company, creating art, or a conversation. Whatever human endeavor we choose, as long as we live our truth, it is success.

The book changed my life. How do you measure that? And that's what true success does — it comes to you in ways you never could have planned, in ways you never could measure, and leaves you feeling grateful. Always.

A N C H O R S

Our minds are creatures of habit. Conditioned patterns, loops upon loops. Most, ironically, seemingly mindless. Most, not helpful.

This is why an anchor is a powerful tool. It uses the nature of the mind. Imagine moments — even if brief — of your mind working for you, rather than against you.

That is the reason why I listen to the same music when I meditate. First, I have positive associations to this piece. And each time I meditate, it returns me to that state. Second, the mind drifts. I have never had a perfect meditation where the mind was still the entire time. But the mind knows this music, its peaks and valleys, and flows with it.

Often, during meditation, as the mind wanders, it's the music that brings it back. Reminds it that it's time to go deep. And sometimes, as the music is ending, I feel my mind panic for a moment, realizing that the meditation is almost over, so it jumps all in. Naturally shifting itself to finish the task it set out to do.

Most importantly, I repeat my truth in my mind, "I love myself," accepting it with each breath. This meditative state, it's the single most powerful way to lay down new pathways in our brain, new synaptic connections that serve us, nourish us from the inside out. It creates progress faster than anything I've ever experienced.

I've started a new anchor at the monastery. In the mornings, I walk outside with my coffee, sip slowly and take in deep breaths, making myself feel love for myself. Five breaths. Sip coffee, love myself, feel it.

In just a few days, I've noticed that all I have to do is go outside with my coffee and my mind naturally shifts to love. Now I'm working to do this each time I drink coffee. Sip, feel love for myself. I'm already noticing the mind slipping into love for myself near the smell of coffee.

I suppose this might make me a coffee addict, but really, it's my mind becoming a love addict. Addicted to loving itself.

It's an addiction I'm more than happy to encourage.

ONE TRUE THING

HEMINGWAY, whenever he was stuck in his writing, would tell himself to write one true thing. A true sentence. Then, he would write another. And another.

It is the best rule I've ever found for writing. Write a true sentence. Something that is real for me. No showing off, no extrapolation, just a simple string of words that equal what I know to be true.

It can apply to anything. Any decision, any fear, any point where we are stuck. Say one true thing to ourselves. And then another. And another. This dislodges the mind unlike anything else.

It's not comfortable, mind you. Truth isn't always. It requires facing fears, standing up to dragons. They are illusions — all fear is — but the only way to overcome them is to face them, say to ourselves: this is what I know to be true. And list it.

I do this sometimes. If I'm stuck, unable to figure out or let go of something, I sit down and write a true sentence after true sentence after true sentence. The beginning is usually messy, as if you're unclogging, but it starts to smoothen, and the truth comes out. Whatever I'm avoiding, whatever I didn't want to admit or was afraid of, it's right there, staring at me in my own handwriting.

And that takes away its power. You feel lighter, you have let it out, and it turns out that the dragon was just a shadow of your mind.

The simple act of putting your truth on paper, only you and your thoughts, it is one of the most powerful exercises you can do.

R E S I S T A N C E

THE *POWER OF NOW* by Eckhart Tolle is one of those books you keep hearing about. I've read it several times. Tried to, actually. Never made it to the end. The last time I picked it up, I didn't make it past the first ten pages. Not because of the content, but because I read something — two words — that, if applied, were the key to freedom.

He was describing his transformation, a night of intense emotional pain, and he heard a voice inside, saying: "resist nothing."

Resist nothing. Like the Tibetan monk who once told me that he found peace by saying yes to all that happened. I met him again years later and reminded him of what he'd said. He laughed.

"Perhaps," he said. "It does fit with my life philosophy."

He had a lightness to him that is rare. His laugh, genuine. I almost expected him to levitate.

If you think about it, how much time do we spend in our heads wishing things were another way, beating ourselves up, beating others up, crafting a different past, wishing for a different future? All of that is resistance. All of that is pain.

Peace is letting it be. Letting life flow, letting emotions flow through you. If you don't fight them, they pass through quickly and you feel better. I think women understand this better than men.

I once took a meditation class where a student asked the teacher how long he had to sit with his suffering for it to pass. He said he'd been sitting with it for over three years.

"That's impossible," the teacher said. "If you really sit with it, it will pass through you in minutes."

Looking back, I understand. Instead of letting it flow, taking him over like a tidal wave that flips you around and around and finally spits you out on the beach, alive and dazed and amazed, he was resisting.

Peace is saying to yourself, "it's ok." Peace is knowing that the maze the mind plays in is not the truth. Peace is knowing that life is. Just is. How we choose to react to it determines our reality.

This is incredibly practical. Not easy, I know. But each time I do it, freedom.

THE POINT

THERE IS SOMETHING MAGICAL about creating. In my case, writing. You start, sometimes with an idea of what will come. Perhaps just a word. Or a sentence ringing in the back of the head. Other times, a blank mind greeting a blank page.

You sit. You stare at the screen, cursor blinking. As an author once said, you cut open a vein, bleed. The more you do it, the more you open yourself, the more you trust the process.

I think it is this way with anything that calls to us, anything that's worth doing. As we trust the process, answers to questions, deep ones, those we never even knew we had or were afraid to ask, they come naturally.

I once heard that Einstein came up with the theory of relativity by imagining himself riding a beam of light. The image of him straddling a shimmering photon and flying through the cosmos, grinning full-on like a child, going "whee!" It made me smile.

One night, I sat down to write. I'd been thinking of someone I loved, wondering what it'd be like to love so deeply, so completely, that you see the other down to their essence. You jump in, become a part of them. Love and galaxies and Einstein flashed in my mind, so I went with it.

I dove in deep, no pausing, no sitting back to think, no editing. I wasn't crafting a story. I was experiencing it and trying to write down what was happening in the moment.

Where the piece took me, I did not expect. In the process came a question — *the question* — and without pause, the answer. It was so simple, so true. But that's the gift of any art. When we go all in, we find the answers. They're in us.

I called the piece, "I see you." It's something I return to occasionally, reminding myself of what I found. Here it is — and I believe that the answer applies to you as well:

"I've been thinking about you," I say.

"Me," you say, the corners of your lips widening. A slow delicious smile. "What about me?"

"Your eyes."

I inch closer. You let me. Your chest rises against mine, falls to my breath.

"Your eyes," I say again, "the freckles and sparkles, sometimes I think that if I stare too long, I'll lose myself."

Your breath deepens. I feel it on my chin, hot. Eyelashes close softly. Eyelashes open. I look at you, your pupils dilated big and open, and suddenly I'm swirling in colors so soft and tender — hazel, brown, green — and then I'm in your iris, it flashing bright and sounding a thump thump and me swimming, my hands parting the optic fluids, warm and silky, and into the long tunnel of your optic nerve.

It spirals like the barrel of a rifle, thunderclouds flashing and booming across neurons, kapow! kabam! — what do you see? What message rushes to your brain? — and curiosity gets the better of me as I swim to the axon of the neuron closest to me, a mass of swirling electricity flashing across the body and tendrils in a sea of dark green. The cell wall parts as I touch it, smooth against my skin as I enter, and closes behind.

I float past enzymes doing their coupling dance. A loose oxygen atom zings past me. I wave at it and continue toward the center. The nuclear membrane folds around me, tumbling me round and round and when it lets go, I'm inside staring at gigantic chromosomes crisscrossing each other like skyscrapers in a mad mad world.

I kick with my heels, gain momentum, shoot inside one, growing smaller and smaller until I see the beautiful double-helix and I stop in awe.

Everything you could be, all that you are, your potential, all encoded in spiraling staircases of molecules. I want to kiss each and every one. Which one expresses itself into your hair? Which one into your laugh?

I float, growing smaller, feeling myself slowly drawn into your DNA, the hydrogen bonds tickling my skin, making the hair on my arms rise, and then whoosh, I'm moving fast, speeding past carbon atoms, still growing smaller, passing oxygen atoms, Van der Waals forces zinging me around like a pinball, and I'm tumbling tumbling falling falling, passing through thick fogs of electrons, feeling the charged hum as they buzz by me, and through black empty space until I see neutrons and protons, glowing purple and violet as they spiral around each other in lazy concentric circles and I slow, growing smaller. Photons whiz by me, large blue balls, and I wait until one is near me and jump on.

"Whee," I shout out as the photon lazily curves through space. A bright light far away grows larger. Neutrinos jump in and out of dimensions around us, little sparkles, some speeding past the photons, going backward in time.

The light grows close, a spiraling galaxy, and I hear a voice, making me almost fall off the photon. I grasp onto it tightly and turn to see God riding a photon to my left.

"Beautiful, isn't it?" he asks again.

God really does have a long flowing beard, robes, the works. He catches me staring at his sandals.

"Got 'em at Nordstrom," he says.

I nod idiotically. He grins, starts to speed toward the light, leaving me behind.

"Wait," I shout. "Wait."

He slows until I'm alongside. We both ride in silence.

"Go ahead," he says gently. "Ask."

I look at him, the galaxy unfurling in front of us. Stars everywhere.

"What's the point," I say. "Of everything. What's the point?"

He smiles. Neutrinos pop around us, fizzle.

"You are," he says finally. "You are the point."

Then he kicks the side of his photon like a bull and speeds off. I watch him turn into a shooting star until it arcs into the galaxy in an explosion of light and then I'm tumbling backward, off my photon, falling and falling, neutrons and protons growing larger, then the humming fog of electrons flipping me around, and then your DNA, your chromosomes, through the nuclear membrane, the cytoplasm, the cell wall, thunderstorms of sodium and potassium ions, and I'm out of the cell, spinning through your optic nerve, your iris, your pupil, and back to you, your breath warm on my face.

"I like how you do that," you say.

"Do what?"

"The way you look at me." You bite your lip. "I feel like you really see me."

I smile, hold you tight. We close our eyes.

COMMITMENT

THE MONASTERY IS BENEDICTINE, an old order dating back to Italy a thousand years. The gift shop has books by Merton, the Pope, the Dalai Lama, Rumi. We are in California.

I leave my cottage and stop in one afternoon, more just to be around other humans. The monk behind the counter — and he looks the part: beard, robe, bald — helps a visitor buy a fruitcake, rings it up on the register, and then answers the phone.

He is smiling, voice nice and gentle. Just as you'd expect. Come to think of it, I haven't run into any surly monks. I'm sure they exist, just not here.

I'm browsing, half-listening, and hear him say several times that "prayer will take care of it." Casually, as if it's the most natural thing. Like me telling someone I'll post a photo on Facebook. In my mind, Facebook is just an everyday reality, no big deal.

And whoa, in his mind, prayer is. The thought stops me: he actually believes this stuff.

I'm often glad others can't hear the chatter in my head. My mind can be rather idiotic sometimes. Of course he believes it. One doesn't shave his head, take a vow of poverty and celibacy, and spend out his life in a robe on a half-dare.

He is at this monastery, committed to, and living what he knows to be true.

If you ask people what they want, often you get the answer: "I want to be happy." But happy is just a bio-chemical reaction. Neurons firing. Chemicals moving from an axon to dendrite to another. Lightning storms of the mind.

Interestingly enough, we often feel that something has to happen for us to give ourselves permission to be happy. A "when I hit this goal, I'll be happy," or "when I have this thing or that person or that level of success, I'll be happy." I've done so much of this. And looking back, I can't think of a less effective way to be.

I think perhaps a better thing to want is fulfillment. A deeper state, one that comes from within, from being your best self. From living life the way you really wish to live it. Then, happiness emanates from within as a byproduct. Naturally.

And how does one live a fulfilled life? By deciding for themselves what is true — whether it's love, faith, commitment to family, a mission, whatever it is — and then living it. Every person I admire who's successful and radiates an inner happiness, they are living their truth.

It's that simple. Decide what your truth is. Then live it.

FREEDOM

Lunch last month with a friend. Cobb salads, iced tea, baseball stadium through the restaurant windows. He'd been on a roll. If you were to chart his trajectory — mental, physical, financial, social, all — his last six months looked like the growth curve companies dream of. Up and to the right. No end in sight.

The guy glowed. Literally. He just got back from the mountains in Utah and had that I-had-an-awesome-sports-commercial-type-of-time look about him. I love having him as a friend, each interaction challenges me to go higher, shows me the possibilities. This day was no different.

I was telling him about the previous week — shutting my company down, dealing with a disgruntled investor, my relationship tailspinning, missing Werner badly — then I launched into how I got through it, how I needed to deepen my practice, and finally my plan to go off to a monastery in a few weeks to get quiet and figure things out.

He smiled and put a hand on my forearm, stopping me.

"How about the pain?" he asked.

"Bugs me," I said. "Last week, there was fear, it kept coming up. And I know better — that's what bugs me, but it still comes around."

He laughed. "You should know better. Of course."

Best things about close friends, they shine the spotlight on the cracks. I could see where he was going, but he surprised me, taking a leap.

"Life is emotion," he said, "life is feeling. If you're not feeling, you're dead." He paused. "Suffering is in the resistance. When we resist the moment."

Suffering is when we resist the moment.

Holy cow, truth.

All suffering is when we say "no," when we say, "I want it another way," when there is no surrender to the present.

"Freedom," he said, leaning back and widening his chest on purpose, "is when we fully open ourselves. To the moment. Experience the moment and let it pass."

I wanted to hug the guy. My mind had been in resistance mode all week, beating myself up for feeling like I should know better. I found myself relaxing, remembering my practice. "It's ok," I said to the worry, to the pain, "it's ok." Accepting it, as I would a child scared by far away thunder. And immediately, I felt myself lighten.

He sensed it too. "See?" he said. "That's all it is. Let it move through you."

We are far far stronger than our pain. It can come in waves, move through us, spice up our life, but suffering, that happens when we fight it, shut the doors and hold off, shouting, "No. You should not be here."

There is no should. There only is. And when you accept that, letting the emotion rise, the feeling crest and crash, say to it, "it's ok. I accept you." Even say to it, "I love you." There is power there. There is freedom.

THE CLIFF

Hollywood is full of beautiful people. New York is full of driven people. Silicon Valley, where I am, is full of smart people. No matter how intelligent you were in your corner of the world, you will find individuals here far smarter than you building companies, coding, slipping you term sheets between drinks. If you want to stretch your intellect, this is a great place to be.

I once asked one of the best entrepreneurs in the Valley how he did it. He's created game-changing companies multiple times. He sort of laughed, then said, "if I only stuck with what I was qualified for, I'd be pushing a broom somewhere."

That sentiment is not uncommon. The best people, they're afraid, they question themselves. Many, if you corner them, will admit that they wonder if they're good enough. But what separates them from the rest is that they jump off the cliff anyway. Sprout wings on the way down.

It's the knowledge — or confidence or hope or sheer stupidity; the word doesn't matter — that they will figure it out. That's it. The only qualification you need to create anything.

First, the desire. Next, the belief that you'll figure it out as you go along. That's what it takes to make the jump. Even if you have to fake it, that's fine.

Besides, here's the simple truth. The one that makes great things happen. Once you're off the cliff and gravity has taken over, you won't have much of a choice.

EFFORT

IF THERE IS ONE LESSON I've learned from failure and success, it's this. I am not the outcome. I am never the result. I am only the effort.

When my last company went down, I crashed along with it. My health, my state of mind, everything. My company failed. But in my mind, I failed. I let down my team, investors, everyone who ever believed in my crazy idea.

Let's step back for a moment. Is that true?

For more than three years, I worked non-stop, first with an idea, then with co-founders who came and went, each time pulling the company forward, never letting it crash, pouring all my savings into it. Seven days a week, and if I wasn't at my desk, I was thinking about work. Nonstop. Not one vacation. Not one weekend off.

The company grew, we closed partnerships, grew revenues. Holy cow, real money! A sales graph of up and to the right. Investors jumped in, seeing the potential that I'd dreamt of years ago. I was close to telling people that we were "killing it," and then…

It blew up. Both engines out, flame on.

As a CEO, your job is to make decisions. Steer the ship, icebergs be damned. Right or wrong is a gift of hindsight, and even then there are biases. The company failed. That was the outcome. And I, with my sense of self attached to the result, believed that I'd failed as well.

In the thick of it, I failed to see the bigger picture. I had to fall to realize an important lesson, one that

I will carry with me in whatever I do: I am not the outcome. No one is. I am my effort, what I put on the table. That's it.

Outcomes are dependent on forces far outside our control. Market dynamics, the price of tea in China, the CEO of Google waking up one morning with an itch to scratch in your vertical. Butterflies fluttering in Japan, tsunamis off the coast of Africa.

What if this book doesn't do as well as the last one? What if it flops? Doesn't matter. What matters is that I'm giving it everything I have. My all. Every single word. I am better for it, and therefore, I believe that you who read it will be better for it.

Success and failure come and go but don't let them define you. It's who you are that matters. And if the outcome doesn't match your desire, you won't crash in the process. Instead, you'll walk away with the lessons learned and go on to create far greater things. Each time, giving your effort. Each time, being your true self.

DEEPER

Louis CK is my favorite comedian. He takes risks, goes inside to uncomfortable places in ways most of us never do. And that's what makes him so good. His honesty, his raw truths.

There is a popular online video of him paying tribute to the late George Carlin. Very worth watching. In it, he talks about his early standup career, the misery of it. He'd been doing the same routine, the same exact hour of comedy, for fifteen years. He hated it.

"I was working at places like Chinese restaurants," he says. "They didn't want to hear me, they wanted to eat."

One night after a show in Boston, he was in his car, feeling like it was all a big mistake, that he wasn't good enough. He put on a CD of Carlin talking about the craft of comedy. What amazed Louis was how Carlin put out a new special every year, a new album, each one deeper than the previous.

"How could he do that?" Louis says. "It made me literally cry that I could never do that — I'd been telling the same jokes for fifteen years."

As if on cue, the interviewer asked George how he created all this new material. Louis almost shook. He leaned in close.

"I hear him," Louis says, "and he says, 'well I just decided every year I'd be working on that year's special and I do the special and then I'd just chuck out the material. And I'd start again with nothing.'"

The look on Louis' face is priceless.

"And I thought: that's crazy! How do you throw away… took me fifteen years to build this hour. If I throw it away, I've got nothing."

A long pause.

"But he gave me the courage to try. This idea that you throw everything away and start again."

With no routine to fall back on, he had to dig inside. He started talking about his feelings. And who he was.

"And then you do those jokes," he says, "and then they're gone. You gotta dig deeper, and you start thinking about your fears and nightmares and doing jokes about that. And then they're gone."

He dug within, layer after layer after layer. What he really wanted to say but was afraid to. At the time, he was a new father and having a tough time at it. So that's what he started talking about, no filter.

"Whoa," he says. "I was somewhere new now."

The original reaction from the audience was shocked laughter.

"But I'd rather have that," Louis says, "than the tepid laughter from my fifteen year old jokes. So I started going down this road."

Fast forward. New specials every year, completely new material, each one deeper and deeper, relevant to who he is at that point in life.

Here's something I've learned about truth. When you first discover and live it, it transforms your life. In no uncertain ways. But it doesn't end there. You cannot stay at the same level as when you first practiced your truth, life won't let you.

Life is entropy. A beautiful chaos. But with rhythm, underpinnings of clockwork. Almost as if designed to push you to the next stage of your growth.

Magic happens, expect it. But challenges come. And when that happens, it's not that your truth failed you or you it. Far from it. This is part of your personal evolution — you need to commit more, you need to go deeper.

Whatever ego you've developed, look hard at it. You will find aspects that no longer serve you. Strip away the layers. Be vulnerable. Be open.

Is this hard? Depends. If you fight it, yes. If you see it for what it is and use it consciously for your growth, you will end up in places that will astound you.

Each time I've fought it, I've suffered. But when I've let go and looked inside to who I am, how I can be better, using my truth as a guide, it's taken me to the next level. A level of amazing growth in such short time that it blows my mind. And my life and finances and relationships show the results.

If you can, make conscious periodic commitments to dive deeper into your truth, into living it fiercely. But if you get lazy and slide for a while, don't worry. The gears are winding. Life will kick in, make you step up.

And when you're standing at new heights, checking out the view, you'll be glad that it did.

R I S E

The greatest achievement of humanity is the human spirit. The ability to rise beyond our circumstances, to find hope in the midst of suffering, to love so deeply that it transforms entire societies.

Gandhi, King Jr., Mandela. The thing that made them powerful was that they knew their truth. It gave them purpose, a vision for change that had to happen and they lived it.

When we work on ourselves, on knowing who we are, what we stand for, what is real — our truth — we have no choice but to live it. And in that process, we will live the greatest version of ourselves.

You and I, we may not transform societies or change the world. Or maybe we will. No way to forecast the ripple effects of our lives. That's like asking an ant on Earth to describe how the planet looks from outer space.

This, I know to be true: the effects our lives have, they are far greater and deeper than we can imagine. We matter, our lives matter. When we live our best selves, we are better for it, the world is better for it. It is that simple.

DAILY PRACTICE

THERE IS NO INTERNET at the monastery. Zero cell reception. An experience of no electronic self. I don't know how else to describe it, but my mind feels sharper.

If there is a piece of the web I could have brought with me, it would be James Altucher's Daily Practice post. I almost believe the Internet was created so that he could write it. He titled it, "How to be the luckiest guy on the planet in four easy steps." It is the most genuine, helpful, and practical blog post I have ever read.

What makes it so powerful is that it's his truth, something that came after hitting bottom again and again. It came from within. Applying it transformed his life.

And James lives it. He's the real deal. It's obvious when you meet him or hear him speak. He's got that inner fire, that spark, that ability to consistently create magic in his life that so many want. And in that post, he's laid out exactly what he does to be this way. It works.

One thing about discovering a truth: first you live it, and after you experience the transformative results, it is real for you unlike anything else. Then you almost become obsessive about sharing it. I think that's why people who discover God or yoga or even a new diet — a way to better themselves — proselytize. It's a fundamental human desire to share what works. And that's good. It propels ideas and over time, moves society forward.

Each time James mentions his daily practice, whether in a new book or a tweet or a post, it makes me happy. It is the biggest public service one can do — show others exactly how to transform themselves, make their lives better. Because when we are better, those around us are better. Ripple effects, far greater than we can foresee.

Bookmark that post, read it once a week. Do the practice. Your life will be amazing.

THRESHOLD

I LIKE TO JOKE that if I knew how well the first book would have done, I would still be writing it. Perfecting it. Like most jokes, it holds an uncomfortable amount of truth.

Instead, I wrote the type of book that I would want to read. Importantly, a book I wish someone had given me when I was down. A book that would have helped me. Then I put it out to the world.

That last step, the crucial one, is where I've seen many talented people stop. They're working away, gathering more data, improving their product, looking for that investor who just gets it, searching for the perfect hire. Everything but hit the submit button. Open the doors, contact the press, announce the company. Cross what I call the threshold.

Once you cross the threshold, you will never be the same. That is a fact.

Creating anything that never existed before is not sanity. Sanity is locking yourself in a box and being fed three times a day. Creating is not safe, it is not risk free. It is putting yourself fully into something that the world will judge. That is madness.

Threshold is where the madness ends and the magic begins.

We all have unfulfilled dreams and goals and desires. Unfulfilled, why? Reasons pop up, but they're just guises for fear. Fear that we're not good enough. Fear that we'll fail. Fear that our fears will be true. Whatever the rationalization is, it is fear. And fear is not the truth.

The truth is that we are mortal, that our time is limited. We must reach into ourselves and do it. We need it more than anyone. And the gift we receive is the person we become in the process.

I think the greatest moments in our lives, the defining ones, they are when we cross this threshold. Take that risk, make that commitment, fling open the door.

Those are the moments we look back at and remember. The moments that make us who we are. The rest of life is just scenery passing by at breakneck speed. But crossing thresholds, those are the crucial plot turns in the movie of our life.

That makes the ride a thrilling one to be on.

AWAKE

In the movie, *Fight Club*, Brad Pitt takes Ed Norton to a small convenience store. Outside, he pulls out a revolver. He is Tyler Durden, the charismatic leader who started their movement. Fearless.

"Whoa, whoa, whoa." Ed is terrified by the revolver. Tries to stop him, ends up following him inside.

Cut to back of store. Tyler drags out a lone terrified employee, makes him kneel. Stands behind him, cocks the revolver. Ed tries to talk him out of it, is brushed aside.

Whoever cast the employee went all out on the stereotype. Chubby, Asian, neat hair, in his twenties, blubbering over himself. Tyler takes his wallet, flips through it.

"You are going to die," Tyler says.

The employee whimpers, cries.

Tyler pulls out an expired community college ID from his wallet.

"What'd you study?"

"S...s...s...stuff."

"Stuff? Were the midterms hard?" Tyler slaps him with the gun. "I asked you, what did you study?"

"Biology, mostly."

"Why?" Tyler asks. "What did you want to be? The question: what did you want to be?"

"Veterinarian!"

"So that means you need to get more schooling."

Hands behind his head, the employee: "Too…too much school."

"Would you rather be dead?" Tyler asks.

"No," the employee says. "Please, no."

Tyler puts the gun away.

"I'm keeping your license," he says. "Going to check in on you. I know where you live. If you're not on your way to becoming a veterinarian in six weeks, you'll be dead. Now, get up, run on home."

The employee runs away, stumbling, fear everywhere. Watching it, I remember thinking, that guy can act.

Ed is beside himself. "That's wasn't funny! What was the point of that?"

Tyler breathes, smiles. "Tomorrow will be the best day of his life," he says. "His breakfast will taste better than any meal you and I have ever tasted."

He hands Ed the revolver, walks away. Ed opens the chamber, peers through where the bullets are supposed to be. Empty.

I think one of the reasons we watch movies is that we instinctually imagine ourselves as the main character, the hero. The one with the secret power. The one who overcomes the obstacle, gets the girl, rides off into the sunset. We are Tyler.

The truth is, we're that poor sad blubbering employee. Living asleep, going through the motions, punching the clock. And then a near miss, a diagnosis, a loved one gone. Kicked awake by Tyler. Kicked awake by life.

Things suddenly are sharper. The question is — and this creates the rest of the story — how long does it last? Do you take that risk, keep that promise you made to yourself that one night under the stars when you were really really happy? Do you go all out?

Or do you fall asleep once again and if you're lucky, Tyler will come knocking.

WHY I WRITE

HEMINGWAY SAID that you write for the one you love. The last book was from a place of giving, written for a dear friend, something that I knew would help. Honestly, up until I hit publish, I was on the fence about putting it out to the world.

I once heard that we all want good judgment, and good judgment is the result of experience, and experience is the result of bad judgment. That made me laugh. In that case, I thought, by now I must be the king of good judgment.

I sometimes think of my past self, the child growing to the man I've become. He doesn't exist anymore except in my imagination. Memories arising when I least expect them. Sometimes, I catch a glimpse of him and I feel such a fondness. I wish I could spare him the pain I know he'll experience. But I also know the love he will experience. The amazing things he'll see, the adventures he'll have.

At the same time, I, who has experienced all that he will, I so often forget the lessons. So I write for him. A guide, perhaps, to the future. To the self that will one day look back and nod, knowing.

After Hemingway finished *The Old Man and the Sea*, the book for which he won the Nobel, he took the manuscript to his wife. She read it, then said to him, "I forgive you for everything."

The act of going within, finding our truth, and then sharing it, it helps us far more than we know. Because when you find that gift and express it to the world, it is better, you are better. It's just the way things are.

That is why I write. To share with the ones I love, to share with myself, to remember and live the lessons, to make fewer mistakes — or at least better ones. A guide for me to return to and apply because I know that when I do, my life flows naturally, things easily resolve themselves. The struggle ceases and magic begins.

THRESHOLD, AGAIN

ONE MORE POINT about the last book. I crossed the threshold, yes. But I did it kicking and screaming, leaving drool and nail marks on the floor. Not a pretty sight.

That book exists because of friends, those I'd shared snippets of writing with. It helped them and they wanted this knowledge out in the world. One checked in on me daily, making sure I was writing. Another created the cover, waiting for the book to be published. After I finished writing and editing, I sat on it. Weeks passed. A month. The fears of what others would think about me if I published it were strong.

Then James Altucher, who had become a close friend and encouraged me to write, scheduled a post on his popular blog about the book and let me know the date. He knew me well enough by this point to understand that there was no way I would let him down. I would publish.

I cannot emphasize enough the quality of those you surround yourself with.

There were others I could have shared the manuscript with. Ones I know would not have been as supportive. Friends in other parts of my life, yes, but a risk like this one, they would have talked me out of it.

Creating something of value, expressing yourself to the world — it is risk. Love is risk. And like love, it is often foolish. Madness even. And like love, it creates some of the most meaningful and fulfilled moments of our lives.

If you're about to take a risk — one that comes from within, one that expresses your true nature, that brings up fear after fear after fear — you know what to do. One: do the work, create the value. Two: draw the people that encourage you closer. They're the only ones that matter.

Others may applaud you after the fact or pull you aside one day at a party and confide that they never could have done what you did. Your job is to smile and remember the ones who helped make it happen. We're human. We flourish in tribes. Odds are, you'll need them again.

If you're reading this book, it means that I crossed another threshold. Faced down more fears, hit submit. Less drool, fewer nail marks.

The lesson from crossing a second time: it gets easier.

CONFIDENCE

CONFIDENCE COMES FROM crossing thresholds. That's it. Once you've done something, made that jump, and even if it didn't turn out the way you thought it would, you've lived and faced fears and are here to tell the tale.

I feel it in writing this book. I know my words matter. Putting the first book out to the world showed me that. What I write now, I question less. Instead, I just focus on making it true, knowing that is all I am required to do.

Whatever area you want to increase confidence in your life, cross the threshold. Do it again and again until it is your norm.

Then seek out other thresholds.

HUMAN

MEALS AT THE MONASTERY are simple: salad, pasta, soup, freshly baked bread. All laid out in the small communal kitchen, the idea being to take your food back to your cottage and eat in silence.

One afternoon, I break convention and eat lunch in the kitchen, stare out through the window to where the hills slope down into brush. Thoughts come and go, memories upon memories. I find myself thinking of my father.

I did not like him. The memories I have of him were of an angry man. When he died, it threw my world off. This, I did not expect.

Even that last night in the hospital with him, when there was nothing left after the cancer but a hollowed shell, I was afraid to reach out, to touch him. Love him. Fear is a powerful thing.

After his death, I could not let go of him, the memories. So I did what came naturally, I ran away from them. I backpacked in foreign countries, not speaking the language, spending days upon days in wilderness.

But memories are faster than you. Emotions, as you push them down, pop up out of new crevasses, faster than you can hammer at them.

A simple realization freed me, mostly. Caused the rocks to loosen, start rolling down. This: he was human. Fallible, full of mistakes, trying to make his way through the world like the rest of us, afraid. Human.

Forgiveness, the key to freedom, followed naturally. I could no longer judge him. He did what he could and he was gone.

Another realization followed. This one, making the rocks disappear. It didn't just free me, it made the concept of freedom unnecessary.

This…

I am human.

Here I am, fallible, judging another fallible being through the lenses of the past, through fear. I thought I had to forgive my father to be free. Turns out, I had to forgive myself. If you come to it that way, forgiveness for others is not just easy, it's a way of being.

I think often we try to save the world, to love others, to forgive them. We think it's others that we need to do something to, something for. The irony is, it's all a path that ultimately brings us to the one who needs it the most — ourselves.

My hope is that with this knowledge, I start with myself first. Always myself. Then, the virtue flows naturally from the inside out.

MOMENTS

WHEN YOU'RE LEANING in to kiss someone you really really like for the first time, the moment is long. When absorbed in a task, short. Moment by moment, our lives are shaped.

I can look at the past regretfully, fondly, wistfully, with as many "lys" as I want, but there is no power there, no truth. Only interpretations for the mind to monkey with. Rather, the only truth is the moment I'm in, this moment, however long it is. And then it is the past and I'm on to this moment.

Moment to moment to moment. I won't succeed most of the time, the gravity of the mind is strong, but whenever I remember the truth, I'm creating something beautiful. A moment where I'm present, where I'm loving myself, nourishing myself.

The irony is that by taking care of myself in this moment, I'm creating a beautiful past for myself as the moment has already passed.

THE SECRET

THERE IS A SECRET. To life, to love, to living your truth, to success in anything.

It's simple too. And in its simplicity lies its power, its effectiveness. Anyone can do it.

The secret is this: pick something that is important to you. One thing. Look at your belief on it, what you know to be true. Then, as if diving off a board, your feet already in the air, you commit.

Sit down, grab a piece of paper, write down what you want to do or be, a vow to yourself. Go all in. The board is already behind you, gravity has taken over, you're falling…

The commitment is the most important part. Not a promise, but deep and from the heart, there is no going back. You have burned the bridges, sunk the ships behind you. This is the only true thing that matters.

Take that piece of paper, put it somewhere you will see it daily. Read it aloud each time you see it, feeling what it would be like to experience that reality. But that is not enough. Do the work.

Do the work. Do the work. Do the work. Do the work. Do the work.

Do. The. Work.

This will transform your life. Do this for fitness, for example, going all in, working out and eating healthy daily and a month later, you'll be amazed at the person in the mirror. Do this for your truth, and you will be so amazing that the world will open doors to you that you never knew existed.

This is the simple secret. Pick something you truly want. Commit. Commit on paper. To yourself. Dive in, do the work. You'll leave the board, falling and falling…until you notice gravity lessen, your rate of descent slowing until it reverses and then…and then, you're flying.

That is the secret.

WHY CREATE?

THE TOOLS HAVE CHANGED, but the process hasn't. You sit, an empty page in front, whether it's pixels or paper or parchment, and you fill it with feelings, with emotion, with life. There is magic here. Real magic.

The world quietly asleep outside the window, the clickity-clack of the keyboard, whatever music I've got on — chill, classical, lounge — and the white of the screen slowly filling.

You dive deeper, you strip away the cleverness and the words become more important than your ego and that's when you know it's real, when it's good. Light spreads out over the hills, covers the monastery. Dawn comes and passes, and a new day begins.

The feeling of when you step away, finished, and you look at the page and you know you tapped into something bigger than yourself, that feeling is, dare I say, spiritual.

THE THINGS I CARRY

As an infantry soldier, I carried everything I needed to survive. Weapon, cold weather gear, ammo, food, water, flashlight, bungee cords. The list would go on forever. My ruck weighed close to as much as I did. And I carried it with pride.

Years later, when I walked from one end of Spain to the other, my backpack held everything I thought I needed on that trip. You learn very quickly the value of a thing. An extra pair of socks carried over a few hundred miles turns into that stabbing pain in your lower back.

By the time I'd walked over five hundred miles to my destination, I'd discarded most of my clothes and possessions. My backpack weighed far less than when I'd started. Extra journals, clothes, mementos, all discarded in garbage cans along the way.

Years later, when consulting and staying in hotels for long periods of time, a large suitcase. Work clothes, going out clothes, gym clothes, laptops, phones, books, work shoes, going out shoes, gym shoes, and on and on.

As I grow older, a simple truth dawns upon me. The things I carry, the things that weigh me down, they are not clothes or furniture or the latest iPhone. Throw any of us on a deserted island, no possessions, we would still be ourselves.

The things I carry are my thoughts. That's it. They are the only weight. My thoughts determine whether I am free and light or burdened. Regardless of whether the world is exploding or celebrating, my inside determines the quality of what I experience outside.

I think that is why many traditions emphasize present moment awareness. Because that takes us away from the maze our brains seem to constantly run around in, slows us down, makes us breathe, and just be. Even for brief moments, just be.

If there is one thing worth working on, it's the inner self. Regardless of the way that works for you, it is the true path. It is where freedom lies.

RIVER

"LIFE IS A RIVER," a wise friend told me. "It's flowing. You're never at the same place twice."

"How's that?" I asked, thinking of mistakes made, patterns repeated.

"Because you're different," he said. "You're changing, growing. Your job is to flow with it. Trust the current. When you relax and go with it, it's easy. But some people," he paused, laughing softly. "Some people, they fight the current, they shout at the river, they paddle up the stream."

I fidgeted uncomfortably, seeing myself doing that.

"And others," he said, "they just start building dams, throwing sticks and stones in the river, trying to stop the flow."

"That's me," I said. "I've definitely done it."

"And how is life then," he asked. "How is it for you?"

"Not so fun," I said.

"Then you know what to do."

BEHIND YOU

I ONCE HEARD SOMEONE describe our fleeting lives as this:

"Look behind you, death is near. Look away. Look back again. Death is closer."

My first career was trauma research in Emergency departments. I've watched more people die than I care to remember. Makes you think. Day after day, going to work, clocking in, putting your lunch in the staff refrigerator, waiting for the next ambulance to arrive. Another patient who woke up that morning, brushed his teeth, put his pants on one leg at a time, not knowing that today would be his last.

Those same pants scissored away later unceremoniously by a tired nurse and thrown on the floor while the trauma team works, inserting catheters and IVs, until the resident stares at the wall clock and calls it.

That idea you had, the company you wanted to start, the book you wanted to write, the song you wanted to sing…

Look behind you. It's closer.

Even if you are one of the lucky ones who gets to do a full tour on this planet. Plenty of time, right? Read up on the regrets of the dying, those in nursing homes. Same, throughout. Not loving enough, doing the shoulds instead of the wants.

Cliché, yes. But clichés exist out of the human experience. Better to listen to them than risk becoming one ourselves.

The truth in life is, we are born, we exist, then we are gone. That's it. What happens before or after is your personal belief, and if you have one, you should live it fully.

But this part — birth, life, death — doesn't matter if you're in a canoe in the Amazon and I'm in a cafe in California, odds are that we'll both agree on it.

Being born and gone, we have no control over. Eventually happens to the best of us. But knowing that one day we will cease, and not knowing whether that is today or a distant tomorrow, that realization is a key to living a fulfilling life.

The trip you wanted to take, the one you wanted to love, the risk you wanted to risk, the movie you wanted to make, the phone call you wanted to dial, the sunrise you wanted to see…

Look behind you. What are you waiting for?

CONSCIOUS

FOURTH DAY at the monastery, the rain returns. I wake up to the sound on the wooden roof. When it lets up, I dress and walk outside to the communal kitchen. The ocean is two colors today: silvery white close to the coast, dark gray where it expands out.

It's the fourth day that I realize why I came here. Werner. He was supposed to visit me this Christmas, had bought tickets earlier in the year. Right now, we'd be hanging out together in my city. Exploring it. Laughing. No wonder I felt the need to get away. To have been there would have been a stark reminder that he wasn't.

That's the hardest part about losing someone. They're gone. Really, really gone.

I stand under the awning outside the building, watch the clouds move in low. They swoop in, skim the top of the chapel. Birds chatter away. Four days and I'm itching to be back home. Sleep in my own bed, wake up and drink my coffee.

Werner was one of the most alive people I ever knew. Women loved him, they couldn't help themselves. His laugh, his smile, his piercing eyes. Guys looked up to him. His wife adored him. If there was anyone who didn't care for him, I have yet to meet them. Not that it would bother him. He knew himself. The opinions of another, unless they were truly close to him, didn't matter.

He had lived life the way he wanted to. That's the most any of us can ask.

The rain builds slowly at first, then hard. I breathe it in. Rain has a smell to it, you forget that living in a city.

I'll leave here in a few days, drive along the coast, return home. There is one thing I'll take with me, a practice of being conscious. Wake up, get my coffee, then go stand outside and breathe the world in. It is a part of me and I of it.

Simple, but sets the tone. Let the mind welcome the day. Then, from that place, start.

Werner would have approved.

HEALING

IT COMES WHEN you find the gift. From the experience, from the pain. There is always a gift. When you discover it, that is when the shift happens, when you taste freedom.

I don't think you can force this. Just be open, let whatever you feel move through you, live your truth, be your truth, and the light flows in. That's really all it is.

FULFILLED

THE MONASTERY IS situated high up in the hills of Big Sur. A two mile road winds down from the entrance to Highway 1. Beyond it, the wide open Pacific. Sunsets were designed for this place.

One evening, I walk down the road. It's cold. I'm wearing thermals and gloves, first time since the Army. The sky darkens quickly. A rabbit jumps out of the bush, startling me. We observe each other for a moment, then it hops back, gone.

I continue down the path. The first star of the night appears. Not gentle, not slowly. One moment not there, the sky barren. The next moment, shining away. Pop! Other stars appear. Pop Pop Pop.

Here I am, warm, lost in my thoughts, while stars and rabbits do their thing. The Mayans were wrong. The world didn't end. It will, someday, for each of us, but it shall be our personal journey, one human following the tracks of countless others.

Life is short. Life is long. Life is. It is whatever we wish to make it be. That is the gift. We may fall, veer wildly off course, make mistakes. You know, being human and all. Makes no difference. Desire and commitment are fundamental human qualities as well, available anytime. A reset is as simple as this moment.

Let's make our time count. Live our best selves. Take the risks, share our dance, belt out our songs. That what we do, even if it's forgotten after we're gone, matters while we're here.

That is a life well lived. A fulfilled life.

LIFE

I RETURN ON THE 30TH, two days early. The after-noon before, while walking and staring at the ocean down below, once I realized why I'd come, I also realized I didn't need to be there any longer. The need just dissolved.

Standing above the Pacific, I knew I wanted to go home. So rather than my standard practice of finishing things no matter what, I just followed the desire. It felt right to do it, so I did. That's all.

Tomorrow, New Year's Eve. I'm not a go out, get crazy type of guy. I'll stay in, reflect over the last week and the coming year. I text a few people I'm back, go to bed, and sleep in late.

I wake up to a text from Jim — my up and to the right friend — he's gotten us tickets to the biggest party in town. Eight DJs, thousands of people. Not exactly what I was looking forward to.

I grab my coffee, call him, and as I wait for him to pick up, remember that Werner was supposed to be at that party. I'd told the promoter, a friend of mine, that Werner would be visiting and he'd offered for Werner to DJ. We'd set it up. I'd forgotten all about that.

Jim gets on the phone and I tell him.

"I would have been there, dancing to his music," I say. "I can't. I just can't."

Jim doesn't miss a beat. No pressure in his voice, just truth. "Perhaps that is the exact place you need to be."

And that quickly, I get it. The very place I was running from, life brought it right to me. I was not supposed to be here, Jim had no idea what the party meant to me, and honestly, until I'd called him, neither did I.

"See you there tonight," I say. "We'll raise a toast to Werner."

I feel him grin through the phone. The beauty of friends, they push you through doors.

That night, we're at the party. Classic New Years, massive, people dressed to the nines. Three floors, eight to ten ballrooms, all thumping. Everyone celebrating, hoping for good things for the coming year. In the end, we're all just human, wishing for simple human things.

Jim gets us two cups of champagne. No glasses here, not exactly what I'd imagined, but it doesn't matter. I go with it, whatever the moment brings. We walk around, section to section and enter a small one, particularly alive, the music thumping, the dance floor busy.

"This is the one," Jim says.

I feel it. We walk to the dance floor, raise our plastic made-in-China cups.

"Make a toast," Jim says.

I realize I hadn't prepared one. I try to think of something good, something special, but only the truth comes to mind.

"To Werner," I say, cup high. "To life."

We touch cups. The DJ is rocking away.

"To life."

The champagne tastes warm and cheap. Werner would have laughed and enjoyed every last sip.

The New Year slides right in.

AFTER

HERE IS WHAT HAPPENS when you get away, break your routine, go silent. At first, nothing. You like it, but a piece of you knows that it's temporary. The memory of home, what you left behind, a constant one.

Three days in, you notice it. Something is different in your head. Something is missing. Thoughts you didn't even know that were pinging at your brain, thoughts you got so used to that they became part of the background. The nonstop radio hiss of life. It's not there.

That bill to pay tomorrow, the groceries to pick up, the email to return, that software to update, the person to call, the appointment to make, the appointment to keep, the appointment to avoid. The day in day out thoughts of living and breathing in the modern world.

Prickly thoughts.

You don't notice them until they lessen. At first, you feel like something's shifted, like when the rain slows down on the roof above. The drip drip drip that your mind was focusing on without even knowing it, almost gone.

And that's when you start to hear yourself. A yourself that you didn't even know could speak. A self that comes from an inner place. Not a voice, but strong feelings and insights physically rising from within your solar plexus up to your head.

They come so quickly, so profound, it's startling. Whatever the issue that you were running from, you get the answer. You'll be walking outside, hands dug deep into your pockets to keep the chill away, and all of a sudden, you just know. From a place so silent and deep, a part of you understands instinctively that if you don't listen, you'll probably regret it.

What about after a retreat? The prickly thoughts return. We've lived a lifetime of these, I don't think they go away that easily. But you carry the gift with you, the insights you received, the knowing that you gave to yourself.

And you return to it in meditation, in walking out under the stars, in creating, in art — anything that requires you to be present in something bigger than yourself.

I used to have these fantasies of going away for long periods, being still, learning from within. But here's what I learned: the insights that we receive when away, they are useless unless we live them. And that happens in the world, with our relationships, our self-expression, our dreams, this crazy beautiful planet we get to walk briefly.

The insights we receive when going silent, it's our gift to ourselves. Returning and living them, sharing them, that is our gift to the world.

G I F T

AFTER THE FIRST BOOK, a few people suggested that I create a series. Love yourself, the workbook. Love yourself, the twelve step program. Love yourself for the ethnic group of the month soul. And so on.

Here's the thing. All I'd done was write down my truth. I was living it, so I could write about it. That distinction is the most important one I've learned.

I recently read a story about Gandhi that crystallized the way I wish to live my life. The story:

A woman comes to Gandhi with her son and says to him, "my son eats sugar all day, it's so bad for his health. He respects you. Can you tell him to stop eating sugar? I know he'll listen to you."

Gandhi looks at her for a moment, thinks.

"Come back with your son in two weeks," he says. "I will tell him then."

The woman is disappointed, but leaves. Two weeks later, she returns, son in tow. Gandhi looks at the boy and says, "stop eating sugar."

"What the…?" The woman's response. "Why did you not tell him two weeks ago?"

"Because before I could tell him to stop eating sugar," Gandhi says to her, "I myself had to stop eating sugar."

I'm just a guy who figured out how to love himself. And if you apply what I discovered to yourself, exploring it from within, it will transform your life the way it did mine. I know that.

Later, I learned that when you're loving yourself and something in life causes you pain, not to fight it. To feel it. Fully. Let it pass through you. That is loving yourself as well. And on the other side, you come out clutching the gift — an open heart.

Walking the Earth with a heart that is open, it is powerful. The love you emanate feels like it could wreck the world, it's so strong. So beautiful. And that creates magic in ways you never could have imagined.

Will I stay this way? I don't know, I'm human. But I know this: I'll work on it with everything I've got. Loving yourself, being open, living fully, it's all a practice. Conscious decisions made and lived each moment. And through it, just like George Carlin taught Louis CK, I shall dive deeper, learn new aspects of my truth. And live them.

I'm starting to believe that our experiences are nothing but a series of gifts and the less we resist them, the better things get. Through the joy, through the pain, through the growth, life is beautiful. I live in a time when I can share my truth across the world with people I will never meet. With the hope that in some way, it creates beauty in their lives. What an amazing gift to me.

LOVE

I PROMISE YOU that the same stuff galaxies are made of, you are. The same energy that swings planets around stars makes electrons dance in your heart. It is in you, outside you, you are it. It is beautiful. Trust in this. And you and your life will be grand.

ABOUT THIS BOOK

Writing, at its best, is a lonely life. Hemingway said that. True. But I think he left something out. Sharing what you have created with the world, it is the most collaborative and life-affirming thing there is.

Nils Parker edited this book with more thoughtfulness than I have ever seen. James, Claudia, Kristine, Sajid, Erin, Tucker, Dawn, Alex — they pushed me across the threshold.

Each one of you that bought the last book, left a review, sent me an email, you showed me that my words matter. And if I learn something of value, no matter how much it scares me to share it, I must. You gave me the courage.

The act of writing, the madness, that is mine. The act of putting this book out to the world, the magic, that is yours.

ABOUT THE AUTHOR

I'VE BEEN FORTUNATE ENOUGH to have some amazing experiences in my life so far. I've trekked to one of the highest base camps in the Himalayas, meditated with Tibetan monks in the Dalai Lama's monastery, earned my U.S. Army Infantry patch, walked 550 miles across Spain, lived in Paris, been the only non-black, non-woman member of the Black Women's writers' group, held the hands of dying patients, and worked with some of the best people in Silicon Valley.

But the most transformative experience has been the simple act of discovering and living my truth: loving myself.

Find me online here:

Twitter: @kamalravikant

Newsletter: http://newsletter.founderzen.com

Please feel free to contact me at k@founderzen.com

I would be honored if you reviewed this book. Thank you.